Foreword

I wish I had had *Success for Struggling Learners* as a resource when I was teaching kindergarten and first grade. I would have referred to it again and again throughout the year and implemented many of the strategies. I certainly will share Peggy's ideas in the work I do now with teachers and suggest that they add this book to their resource library.

We have always had students who need alternative teaching strategies in order to develop as successful readers and writers, but as Peggy states, each year we seem to be meeting more and more of them in our classrooms. It can be a daunting task to provide successful learning strategies for everyone, and yet as teachers we are committed to helping all our students do their very best.

Peggy gives us a myriad of simple ways to respond to all these children. She tells us how to be attentive to the lighting in our classrooms for optimal visual discrimination, suggesting that some students may need to wear baseball hats or visors to cut down on glare. She recommends providing earphones for the child with auditory processing difficulties. She offers easy exercises to establish hand dominance and others to strengthen the palmer arch, necessary for writing and other fine motor activities. She encourages us to make hands-on activities part of our daily routine, especially for tactile and kinesthetic learners, and she shows us sensible ways to address the needs of hyperactive students. She demonstrates how to help nonverbal and shy students become active participants in the classroom, and how to teach struggling learners to develop organizational and book-handling skills.

The suggestions in this book, however, do not apply only to struggling learners. Many will benefit all students, and Peggy wisely suggests that when introducing a new strategy aimed at a specific student, we present it to the entire class as well and allow all the students to try it. After all, what kindergartner wouldn't want to use a pair of "binoculars" in order to focus on something special around the room? What first grader wouldn't want a piece of colored acetate to put over his or her book to see the print more clearly? What child wouldn't enjoy learning sign language?

Peggy speaks as a loving, caring teacher who believes in her students as learners and as human beings. She also draws from her own personal experiences as the parent of a struggling learner, who has worked with her daughter's teachers to develop the successful strategies in this book. The gift she gave to them she is now giving to us.

Bobbi Fisher
Author and educational consultant

Preface

My first two books, *I Teach Kindergarten* and *Tricks of the Trade*, were written from the head. My teaching knowledge, expertise, and experience seemed to just pour out of my head and onto the pages. This book, however, was written from the heart because one of my three children is a special needs child. Through her trials, tribulations, and triumphs in learning, I have become a better person, a better mother, and a much better teacher. What she and I have learned together is the basis for this book.

I have always wanted a lot from life, but the top two things on my list were to become a teacher and to be a loving mother. God blessed me with both. I have three wonderful children and two of them were given the gift of being able to sit in a classroom day in and day out and learn with ease everything that is taught. On the other hand, my oldest child struggles day in and day out in her educational world. She is a hands-on learner in a world that values children who sit and listen to a teacher lecture. She needs to see and do rather than listen, listen, listen. She needs extra time to process information, and she needs teachers to commun-icate in differential ways to accommodate her style of learning.

I am continually in awe of how she negotiates her world and always puts forth 110% effort even when she is faced with failure, defeat, and discouragement. She will go far in life because she is doggedly determined in everything she does. Her struggles have been many, but we have always been blessed with great teachers who have gone the extra mile with her.

This book is written for the teachers who are faced with children who struggle in the regular education classroom—those sweet little souls who may be asking themselves, "Why can everyone else do it but I can't?" If one of these ideas helps even one child struggle less, then my efforts have been worthwhile.

It takes a gifted teacher to see life through the eyes of a child who struggles and to truly understand how hard it is to survive in a classroom where he or she learns differently from everyone else. This book is a compilation of material drawn from years of trying to help my daughter, to support the teachers who teach her, and to help the students I have been blessed to educate.

It has been a remarkable and rewarding journey.

Peggy Campbell-Rush

Introduction

Those of us who are regular education teachers are encountering more and more special education students in our classrooms and we are often ill equipped to help them. We also may have many students who are yet undiagnosed as having special needs. Then there are those who just need an extra measure of intervention from the regular education teacher. Consequently, we are faced with teaching and helping all children no matter what challenges they present for us in the classroom. That's the purpose of this book—to provide a variety of ways you can help struggling learners have a wonderful, calm, exciting, nurturing, secure, and successful launch into the world of education.

I have one rule of thumb when I introduce a new technique intended for a particular child who is struggling: I let each of my students try it out. As you know, all the children will be intrigued by any change in the daily routine and they will all want to investigate anything different that's being suggested to another student. I find, however, that the dust settles quickly and only the student who really needs the new twist or trick will use it in the end. I also discuss openly with the students why I am using this with one of their classmates. Speaking with words that students can understand, I explain that we are all different and sometimes we need help that will make learning the best it can be. I have found students are remarkably understanding, compassionate, and resilient when I do this.

We teachers need to have a number of "tricks" up our sleeves that we can pull out and give a try. If any of those included here do not seem to be working, move on to others. You just may hit one that helps a student become a lifelong learner and experience the utter joy of learning.

As you work with your students, and especially those who struggle, try to remember the following:

- Make directions multisensory: auditory, visual, and tactile.
- Coach active listening: sit still, look at the speaker, and watch facial expressions.
- Children are distracted by the most stimulating thing in the room: BE THAT! Find the carrot that the child will work for and dangle it often.

Visual Discrimination

Too much visual stimulation can be very confusing and upsetting to struggling learners, and makes it difficult for them to focus on a given item or lesson. This doesn't mean you have to turn your entire classroom into a bare and boring space, but do keep simplicity in mind for an occasional display and center area. As the year progresses, reassess the overall environment from time to time, making sure it accommodates the visual needs of all your young learners.

◇ Hats On

Fluorescent lights have different effects on different students. Some find them to be a depressor and others, a stimulant. If you notice that a student is having trouble focusing on a page, paper, or work item, try moving him or her near a natural source of light like a window. If that is not an  option, give the student a baseball cap or a sun visor to cut down on the glare. I also allow students to work under a table where there is sufficient light but no overhead glare. This may calm a student who is overstimulated by the lights.

◇ Boys Are Longitude

Boys are optically programmed to view print in a vertical manner. This is why you see them writing one word on each line rather than a string of words across the page. Many boys will benefit from "feeling" return sweep (which is reading or writing that goes across a line of print and loops down to the next line). I either buy an extra copy of a favorite book or have children illustrate a story on paper. I then take the pages and mount two-thirds of the story along the wall with the remaining one-third of the pages below that line. I have the boys walk and talk the story. When they get to the end of the first line they crouch down and move to the beginning of the next line and finish telling the story. This technique can be used with girls, too, if you find they need practice in a kines-thetic way. Girls are more latitudinal in the optical focus and have an easier time with return sweep.

◇ Wear the Word

Save the name-tag holder you get at your next teacher in-service or conference. Remove the paper with your name on it and slip in a card that has the letter of the week or word of the day written on it. Wear it and ask the students every so often what it says. Struggling learners will need to see a word, letter, or shape at least 20 times before they can begin to recall it.

◇ Color Switch

Black print on white paper works well for most of the students in our classrooms; however, there are those who focus better if other colors are used. Try a red marker on yellow paper and other color combinations to see if they have any effect on the student's ability to focus on their paperwork. Use a different colored marker when you write sight words on a chart too, which helps the student focus in on frequently used words.

◇ Lined vs. Unlined

The use of lined or unlined paper can lead to heated discussions among teachers in primary classrooms. So I leave the decision to the children. I provide all kinds of lined and unlined paper and let each child choose what suits him/her best.

◇ Placemats

Ask your struggling learners to select the piece of colored construction paper that they like best and to lay it on their desk. The students can then place their workbook, work sheet, or other paper on top so that the colored paper serves as a frame and helps them focus on their work space.

IDEA TO TRY:

Remember that some students do not have the ocular control that is necessary to copy from the board until age eight. Provide a mini-version of word walls, number lines, and alphabet charts that a student can place on his/her desk to copy from or refer to. See page 20 for instructions on making Wandering Word Walls.

◇ Binoculars

Take two empty cardboard toilet paper tubes and tape them together to form a pair of "binoculars." The student puts the binoculars up to his/her eyes and focuses only on the area you want him/her to see. All the peripheral areas will be blocked from the student's line of vision. If you make a small hole on the outer

side of both tubes, thread through a string, and knot both ends, the binoculars can hang around the student's neck until the next time he/she needs them.

 ## Color Overlays

At stationery shops and office supply stores, like Office Depot or Staples, buy a variety of color overlays, which are thin pieces of acetate the same size as an 8 ½" x 11" sheet of paper. When the student places the overlay on top of what he/she is reading, the print immediately becomes clearer. Try yellow first; it is very soothing and students react well to it. Then let the child choose his/her favorite color and watch for the reaction. You can cut the overlays to any size you need.

 ## IDEAS TO TRY:

Depending on his/her needs, allow a student to sit close to you or farther away in order to be able to focus properly.

Avoid teaching a difficult academic task where there is a distracting background.

◇ Divide and Conquer

Often a full work sheet or workbook page is overwhelming for a struggling learner to confront, but when it is divided into smaller parts, it becomes quite manageable. Cut away one quarter of a piece of oak tag and use it to frame the section of the paper or page you want the child to work on first.

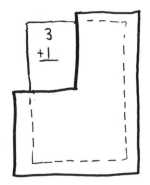

Start with the top left quarter of the page uncovered. Rotate the oak tag clockwise by 90° to work on the top right quarter, rotate it another 90° to work on the bottom right quarter, and another 90° for the bottom left.

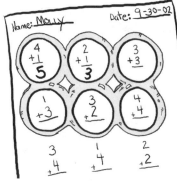

to

Some teachers use the plastic rings from a six-pack of soda cans to frame sections of a paper for a student to work on. You also can simply fold a work sheet vertically so the child works on only one column at a time.

◇ Lift Off

Another way to help students focus on specific skills is to write on the overhead projector and project what you've written onto the screen. Then tell your students that you are going to remove the word or words from the screen. Take a white paper plate or white piece of cardboard and place it over a word on the screen. Slowly walk the paper forward, away from the screen. The word seems to move right off the screen. This mesmerizes the students and everyone wants to see the magic happen again and again. Each time the students focus on a word, they are visually imprinting that word and will have an easier time recalling it in the future.

IDEAS TO TRY:

Make sure that boards are wiped clean. Powdery backgrounds can distort the clarity of written letters, words, or numbers.

Schedule a few minutes for the students to close and relax their eyes.

Do some visual tracking exercises. Have the student watch an object while you slowly move it up/down and left/right.

◇ Beginning, Middle, End

Some students find it overwhelming to look at an entire alphabet chart, so I underscore parts of it with brightly colored masking or highlighting tape. I use green to show the beginning of the alphabet (A-I), yellow for the middle (J-R), and red or pink for the end (S-Z). So, when a student is looking for the letter "T," for example, I can direct his/her attention to the end of the alphabet above the red tape. This also is a pre-dictionary skill for our youngest students as they begin to learn to segment the alphabet.

Aa Bb Cc Dd Ee Ff Gg Hh Ii Jj Kk Ll Mm Nn Oo Pp Qq Rr Ss Tt Uu Vv Ww Xx Yy Zz

◇ Wandering Word Walls

While many of your students will be able to focus on and use the words you have mounted on your word wall, students with visual discrimination difficulties won't be able to focus. These children need the words to be on the same plane or, in other words, right in front of them. For this situation, I developed "Wandering Word Walls." Here are two types:

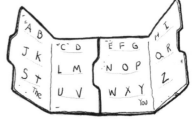

1. Open two center-cut file folders and lay them flat. Fit them together like a puzzle and secure them with tape.

Take an alphabet strip and cut it into thirds: A-I, J-R, S-Z. Tape the first third of the alphabet strip across the top of the folders—or print the letters, if you prefer. Attach the second third of the strip across the middle and the last third near the bottom. As you add words to the word wall mounted in your classroom add the same words to your wandering word wall. This can be placed upright on a student's desk, providing a great resource at eye level and even serving as a "privacy shield" for a child to do some quiet work.

2. Cut your alphabet strip into thirds or write the alphabet (A-I, J-R, S-Z) on three separate pieces of oak tag. Tape a blank sentence strip or piece of oak tag under each third of the alphabet, connecting them all together with tape. Mount this on a coat hanger and hang it from a doorknob or hook in the classroom. Students can retrieve the word wall and use it at their desks as needed. I use a green sentence strip for the beginning third of the alphabet, yellow for the middle, and red or pink for the end.

 Spacing

Students with visual discrimination difficulties have trouble leaving spaces between words when they write. Try this fun and simple solution. Using a tongue depressor or Popsicle stick, show them how to place it on the paper after writing a word and then make a small dot where the new word should begin. A fun alternative is to glue two Popsicle sticks together, narrow side to narrow side. (Reinforce with book-binding tape if needed.) Attach a fake fingernail to the ends of both sticks to show "two-finger" spacing.

I also use tongue depressors with a google eye glued to the top end so students can use them to "keep their eye on the words" as they track under the printed text in a book.

IDEAS TO TRY:

Use bright white paper and a thick black marker when writing in front of the class.

Organize bulletin boards to focus on one particular thing.

Use the overhead projector to teach.

◇ Frame It

To help a student zero in on a specific word or phrase on a page of print make some "framing devices."

~ Take a piece of oak tag and cut out a square or rectangular shape from the center to create a frame. Make several of varying sizes.

~ Cut the center out of a flyswatter so students can swat and frame a word.

~ Cut off the front side of a bill envelope that has the cellophane see-through window and use that as a frame for words and print.

◇ Eye Aerobics

If we are to expect struggling learners to be able to track print on a page, we need to help them strengthen their eye muscles. A fun way is by doing what I call "eye aerobics." We all hold up our pointer finger and, without moving our head, we follow the movement of our finger with just our eyes. We look right at our

own finger as we slowly move it up and down, from side to side, and diagonally from top to bottom and bottom to top. One set is enough but make sure your movements are slow and steady.

◇ Be a Star

When I want the students to focus on me or I need to grab their attention, I turn on the overhead projector. Then I put on my sunglasses and stand in front of the lighted screen. All eyes are riveted on me as though I were a Hollywood movie star!

◇ Highlight

Often there are a lot of peripheral details or illustrations on a page that can be distracting to a child. To help focus the child's attention on the most important information, highlight it with a brightly colored marker. Highlighting tape works well too.

IDEAS TO TRY:

Turn off a bank of overhead lights and invite the student to sit on the side of the room that is most comfortable for him/her.

If possible, sit a student near a natural source of light, as fluorescent lights can cast a glare.

Place the child away from areas that have an overabundance of visual stimulation, like a computer monitor or brightly colored bulletin board.

Auditory Processing

Students who have auditory processing difficulties are hypersensitive to noises, do not hear well, or do not learn easily through listening. Since much of what we do in the classroom relies on a student's ability to process auditory directions, the struggling learner who depends solely on visual or kinesthetic learning is clearly at a disadvantage. Here are some teaching techniques to try with these children.

◇ Mime It

Go through the steps of a project like a mime, using no words, and ask the student to verbalize what he/she thinks you are doing. (Correct him/her as necessary.) For example, get two pieces of paper, some glue, and a pair of scissors. Take these to the child's desk or table and sit down with them. Write your name on one of the pieces of paper, cut out a shape, glue it on the other paper, and put this in your teacher's basket. If this proves to be too many directions for a young child to follow, break them down into sets of two or three steps at a time.

◇ Earphones

For some students our classrooms are simply too noisy. These children are overwhelmed by the sounds, even when we feel the room is relatively quiet. I keep two different types of earphones on hand for these students. One type is from a classroom tape player: I cut the cord off a few old sets of earphones that went to it. They allow sound to filter through but not at the volume the rest of the class hears it. The second type is the kind used on airport runways, or by hunters, available at most sporting goods stores. These earphones block out all sound so you will have to tap a student on the shoulder to get his/her attention. They are especially handy when a child has to do independent reading or other work but the noise level is too distracting. Winter earmuffs, a headband, or coat hood belonging to the student also works well to filter out noise.

◇ Sensory Overload Space

Some students need to get away from the noise and activity in the classroom for a few minutes or they will become overstimulated. To remedy this situation, I made a private space out of a washer/dryer box. I cut off the top flaps and tacked carpeting samples on all

the inside surfaces. Then I turned the box on one side, moved it to an out-of-the-way spot in the classroom, and equipped it with a pillow, flashlight, and a few books. This provides a comforting and quiet refuge where a student can sit and regroup or rest for a few minutes before rejoining the rest of the class.

IDEAS TO TRY:

Provide the student with a pair of personal earplugs to cut down on the volume of noise in the classroom.

Set up an area of your room where it is carpeted, which helps to muffle the sounds of the classroom. This is especially useful when the student is trying to read a book.

 ## Sing and Learn

Singing and putting words to music helps all students learn more easily, but this is especially beneficial to struggling learners. You can write words or concepts on a chart and then make up a song to teach them, using a familiar tune like "Old MacDonald Had a Farm" or "Twinkle, Twinkle Little Star." Ask your grade-level colleagues to help. Each person can come up with one song to teach a concept at your grade level. This is actually a lot of fun for everyone!

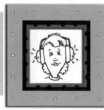

◇ One More Time

We're all familiar with the statement, "If I've told you once, I've told you a thousand times." For students with auditory processing difficulties, you WILL have to repeat things many—if not a thousand—times to help them remember because listening is not their strong suit. Keep at it and remember that repeated exposure to listening for details will help the student cultivate strategies for lifelong learning.

◇ Laugh and Learn

Humor increases retention of information, makes learning fun, and creates smiles all around. And it doesn't have to be vocalized in order to be funny. If a student can remember the humor, he or she will remember the information that went with it.

◇ Say It Again, Sam

Question the relevance of the information you are presenting. What is the MOST important thing to learn and remember from the lesson you are teaching? Point out specific information to a student with auditory processing difficulties, then have the student repeat what you said so you can be sure that what he or she heard is indeed what you were saying. This ensures that the most important information will be foremost in the student's mind.

◇ Picture This

Students with auditory processing difficulties need strong visual clues or cues to go with verbal messages. I take photos of routines that we do in class, mount them on poster board, and place this where the action is expected to occur. For example, next to the coat cubbies there are pictures of a student taking off his or her coat, placing the coat on a hook, taking off his or her backpack, taking out a folder, and hanging the backpack next to the coat. Above the box where we store our glue bottles there is a picture of a student tightening the glue top and placing it upright in the glue box. This enables the student who has difficulties processing what I say to literally see what I mean. (Be sure to find out first what your school district's policy is regarding photographing students.)

◇ Story Talk

Students with auditory process-ing difficulties need to "see" a story to help them with their comprehension of it. Before the student begins to write, I initiate "story talk" with the child, and he/she talks out the story he/she wants to write. I then go to the computer and type what the student tells me. I ask the student to read it back to me (with help if needed), and then the child can write his/her own version of what was said. This gives lots of rehearsal for writing and I have a record of what the student wants to write if he/she gets off track.

IDEAS TO TRY:

Minimize auditory competition by speaking only when there is relative quiet in the classroom. Don't shout over the children or give directions when the morning announcements are being broadcast over the loudspeaker.

Provide the student with a Phonics Phone, which enables him or her to hear the words and sounds he/she says and to learn how to say them correctly. (These are available through Crystal Springs Books: 1-800-321-0401 or www.crystalsprings.com.)

◇ Body Language

Vary the pitch and tone of your voice when you teach and alter or change the response modes from the children too. This keeps everyone interested to see what comes next. When asking students to repeat information, you can have them sing it like an opera singer or say it like they are underwater or have just run 10 miles. You can also have them indicate responses nonverbally. For example, they can cross their legs for YES and uncross them for NO, or signal with thumbs up for YES and thumbs down for NO, or place their hands on their head if they think the story we are reading is fictional and hands on their hips if they think it is factual.

◇ Listen Up!

Forewarning students that they really need to listen closely because something very important is about to be said helps those with auditory processing difficulties. You can cup your hand behind your ear in an exaggerated stance or hold up a picture of a giant ear to give students the cue to "listen up!"

◇ Tap and Talk

When giving directions, hold up the same number of fingers as there are steps involved, then ask the student to hold up the same number of fingers. For example, for a three-part direction ask the student to hold up three fingers. You might say, "I want you to go to your seat, take a pair of scissors from the basket, and cut out this  circle." As you say each direction tap one of the student's fingers. Then hold up three fingers, have the student repeat the directions, and tap each one of your fingers as he/she states each one. That way you can check to see if you are overloading this student with too many verbal instructions at a time. If the student can repeat only two directions, have him/her do the first two steps and then come back to you so you can repeat the second set of directions with this "tap-and-talk" method of instruction.

IDEAS TO TRY:

Use simple, short phrases when talking with these students.

Give visual clues or tactile demonstrations for directions rather than auditory ones.

◇ Watch Your Words

For a student with auditory processing difficulties, what you say may not be interpreted as you intended. For example, after a lesson on long and short vowels, I heard a student say that "the long vowels look pretty short too"(!). I have to be careful that what I say doesn't have a double meaning that could be confused or misconstrued. Many of these students also have trouble with jokes so be aware of how you handle humor, too.

◇ Silent Reading

For some students, silent reading is anything but silent. Often they have no idea that they are reading out loud and bothering others. Encourage them to put their finger on their lips as they read and tell them that if their lips are moving, they are reading out loud. If they still can't do it silently, let them read with a puppet. I tell them that only the puppet is allowed to hear them so they have to speak very softly and hold the puppet close to their face. This way the puppet will block and absorb some of the sound and the student will speak in a quieter voice.

◇ Wait Time

Be aware that the time it takes for a struggling learner to hear a question, process the information, formulate an answer, and respond will be much longer than for a child who does not have difficulties. Normally it takes children three to seven seconds to respond to the teacher. Struggling learners can take over a full minute for a girl and three to four minutes for a boy. Make sure you allow plenty of time to listen to a student who finally has the answer to a question that you asked earlier.

Small Muscle/ Fine Motor Control

Many students struggle with writing tasks because they cannot hold a pencil, marker, or crayon correctly, or they cannot write or color with any degree of accuracy or satisfaction. In addition, they may be unable to hold and cut with scissors. If you have students struggling in these ways, there are two things to remember:

First: "If it ain't broke, don't fix it." In other words, if the way the child holds a pencil looks unorthodox to you but he/she can control and manipulate writing and cutting tools with a degree of success, then don't waste your time—or the student's—trying to correct this. You have better things to do and to teach. I have had many students in my classroom with seemingly impossible pencil grips who have done fine with all their work. If a student, however, cannot get work done and becomes frustrated because he/she cannot get control of the writing implement or scissors, *then* it is time to intervene with some hands-on instruction.

Second: Small muscle coordination and fine motor control in the fingers and hands actually starts in the upper arm. All muscles from the shoulder to the fingers need to be strong to improve a pencil grip or scissor hold. This chapter focuses on a variety of exercises, games, and techniques to use for increasing muscle strength and motor control.

◇ Palmer Arch

Ask your students to hold out the hand they write with, palm up, and straighten the hand. Look at the palm and you will see what is called the palmer arch. Students with good hand-writing and cutting abilities will have a dip in their palm; those without these skills will have a flat palm. Doing strengthening exercises for this part of the hand will develop the palmer arch and result in better control for the student.

◇ Spill the Beans

This is a good exercise to develop the palmer arch. Open a bag of dried navy beans and spill them out onto a tray. Have your students use a black marker to make two dots for eyes on each bean so it looks like a ghost. Ask the students to pick up a bean, using their thumb and pointer finger, drop the bean into the palm of the same hand, and hold it there using the three remaining fingers. Then the "pincer grip" fingers (thumb and pointer finger) try to pick up another bean, drop it in the palm, and so on. Students should start with their dominant hand (the hand they write with), but this is a good exercise for the other hand too. Some students will have to sit on one hand so it doesn't try to help the other one.

◇ Tennis Anyone?

Take an old tennis ball and cut a two-inch slit into it. Have the student wrap his or her hand around it and squeeze. The slit will open up and look like a mouth. Draw two dots above the slit to look like eyes. Then ask the student to "feed" the ball by dropping bingo chips, marbles, or pennies in the "mouth" each time he/she squeezes it. When the tennis ball gets filled up, the student squeezes it again and "coughs" all the items out of the ball's mouth!

◇ Get a Grip

For another palmer arch exercise, roll up a paper towel or piece of aluminum foil into a small ball, or use a cotton ball. Put it in the student's palm and ask him/her to hold it with the last two fingers. Then have him/her grip a pencil with the other three fingers. Holding the ball will use the palmer arch muscles and allow the student to have a tripod grip on the pencil.

◇ Arch Supports

Buy a Styrofoam egg or ball about
the size of a golf ball or ping-pong
ball. Take a pencil and push it
through the top third of the ball. Have
the student wrap his/her hand around
the ball and then hold the pencil, using
the tripod grip. If the Styrofoam is too
slippery to hold on to, use a practice golf
ball or a whiffle ball, which is a small plastic ball punched
with holes. Slide a pen through the top third (I use a pen because a pencil needs to be sharpened too often and is hard to
remove), and as before, have the student wrap his/her hand
around the ball and then hold the pen, using the tripod grip.

◇ Sock It Away

To help a student keep the last two fingers of
the hand out of the way when gripping a
pencil I make him/her a "cast." I take a
child's clean white sock and cut a hole
in the toe area for the pointer and
middle fingers to stick through. I cut
another hole in the heel area for the thumb
to stick through. The student slides his/her
hand into the sock and curls the last two fingers
into the palm, where they stay inside the sock. The
other three poke through to create a tripod grip.

◇ Cracking Up

Get a few nutcrackers, gather some twigs, and set out a cookie sheet. Then let the students crack the twigs with the nutcracker over the cookie sheet to their hearts' content. Clean up is easy as you simply take the cookie sheet to the trashcan, drop in the cracked twigs, wipe down the tray, and start all over again.

◇ That's the Last Straw

For this activity you need a box of plastic straws, a shoebox, a pair of scissors, string, and/or pipe cleaners. The student cuts a straw over the box and keeps trying to cut the pieces smaller and smaller, making sure they all fall into the box. Then he/she takes the little straw pieces and threads them on a string or pipe cleaner to make a bracelet. (Precaution: Do not let the student make a necklace out of these pieces as there is a potential danger of choking.)

◇ Paper Chase

Sometimes a student is not able to keep his/her paper from moving while writing or coloring. This can be upsetting and distracting for a young child. An easy solution is to secure the paper to the desk with a little tape.

◇ Making the Cut

Many times a student without a strong grip has trouble cutting with scissors. To compound the problem, the paper to be cut may be too flimsy for the child to hold in position. In this instance, I tape or glue the worksheet or paper to a piece of construction paper, making it stiffer, sturdier, and easier to hold and cut.

◇ Light Handed

Place a piece of fine-grit sand-paper under a work sheet or paper so that the student uses the muscles in the hand to control the pencil, crayon, or marker being used. This also keeps the student from pressing down too hard when writing or drawing, which can tire the hand after a few minutes.

◇ Choices

Paper for the primary grades generally has widely spaced lines, which may be difficult for some students to use, so keep various sizes of lined paper on hand. I provide students with unlined paper as well, and let them experiment to discover which works best for them.

◇ Finger Gymnastics

While the students and I are standing in a line waiting to go somewhere, we sometimes do finger gymnastics. We raise our arms and put our fingers near each other. Then we make up things to do with our fingers, like play soccer (the fingers pretend to kick a ball), jump rope (the fingers spin round and round each other), play basketball (the fingers pretend to bounce a ball and shoot it high), and whatever else we come up with to do.

These are fun ways to exercise and strengthen hand, arm, and shoulder muscles.

◇ Vroom! Vroom!

My students and I practice wrist
control and strengthening exercises by
pretending to ride a motorcycle. We
put our hands out in front of us and
turn our wrists up and down to speed
up and slow down the motorcycle. We
hang on as we turn corners and, of
course, make the appropriate motorcycle sounds!

◇ Slant the Surface

Some students have
weak wrists and need a
way to provide wrist
control. You can do this
by slanting the surface
they write on. Purchase
"slant-boards" from
school supply catalogs or

make them yourself. For maximum control
take a 3" three-ring binder and place the child's paper on it,
anchored down with a piece of tape. As the student gains more
wrist strength, you can provide a smaller (2") and smaller (1")
binder.

◇ Lying Down on the Job

Occasionally students will need full arm support in order to use a pencil or pen and write successfully. Allow them to lie on their stomachs on the floor and rest on their elbows. With the upper body propped up, all the arm muscles are supported, which makes it easier for them to control the wrist, hand, and finger muscles.

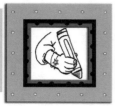

IDEAS FOR STUDENTS TO TRY:

The following activities will be beneficial for strengthening small muscles and increasing fine motor control.

~ *Turn a jump rope.*

~ *Squeeze a stress ball or water squish ball.*

~ *Use a single-hole punch, tweezers, tongs, turkey baster, and nutcracker.*

~ *Knead and roll Play-Doh.*

~ *Use pencil grips.*

~ *Practice holding and using pencils, pens, crayons, and markers of different sizes and shapes.*

~ *Play games like tug-of-war, practice throwing and catching balls or beanbags, and simply have fun spraying with plastic spray bottles.*

~ *Screw and unscrew jar lids. (This works on the three-finger tripod grip.)*

~ *Type on an old manual typewriter (if you can find one) or on a computer keyboard.*

~ *Practice woodworking skills like hammering nails but make sure safety glasses are on!*

~ *Trace around stencils (both the outside and inside).*

~ *Use an eyedropper to collect water and drip it out into a cup.*

~ *Swing on a swing set.*

~ *Stick some clay onto the eraser end of a pencil to weigh it down so it rests in the space between the thumb and pointer finger.*

Hand Dominance

By the time students enter school, most have established their hand dominance: they are either right-handed or left-handed. A few, however, switch their pencil, marker, or crayon from hand to hand as they write or draw from one side of the paper to the other, which may indicate that their hand dominance has not been determined. If this is the case, these students will benefit from doing exercises to help discover their dominant side.

Always conference with parents first, however, to get their input on this issue. Sometimes you will find out that the parent did not establish his or her own hand dominance until a later age. I also ask the parent which hand his/her child appears to favor at home and if the parent has any suggestions about which hand should be the dominant one.

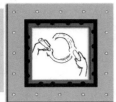

◇ Left or Right?

When trying to determine a student's dominant side, I use the strategies that follow. Once I have determined which side seems to be the more dominant, I make sure the student holds a pencil, marker, crayon, etc. in the hand on the dominant side when doing work.

~ Have the student try to screw and unscrew a jar lid, and watch to see which hand is more dominant or has more strength.

~ Roll a ball straight to the student, trying to keep it from veering to one side or the other, and ask him/her to try to kick it. Do this about 10 times in a row, watching for which foot strikes out to kick the ball more often. This will be the dominant side.

~ Give the student a piece of paper with a line drawn vertically down the center, plus a marker, crayon, pen, or pencil. Ask him/her to make dots on the left side of the line with the left hand and on the right side with the right hand. Examine the paper to see which side has the darker dots, indicating that the student pressed harder.

~ Give the student a camera and ask him/her to take pictures. Note which eye the student focuses with more often.

~ Ask the student to put both hands by his or her side. Stand in front of him/her about 4 feet away and throw, underhanded, a soft cloth ball straight to the child, toward the center of the

body. Ask the student to try to catch it or bat it away with only one hand. (It is not important whether or not the student catches or hits the ball each time.) Do this about 10 to 20 times in a row to see which hand comes up most often.

◇ Start at the Top

Remember that finger control, pencil grip, and small muscle control develop after large muscle control has been established (see Small Muscle/Fine Motor Control, page 35). To strengthen the arm, you need to start at the shoulder and work down. Increased upper arm strength will, in turn, increase fine motor control. Do lots of large movements like writing and drawing on the blackboard, painting large murals, and doing exercises like Finger Gymnastics (see page 41).

IDEAS FOR STUDENTS TO TRY:

Play Simon Says and cross one arm over to the opposite shoulder and repeat with the other arm and shoulder.

Walk along a line drawn on the ground, crossing the left foot over to the right side of the line and the right foot over to the left side.

Paint a large mural with broad strokes back and forth across the paper.

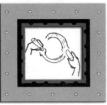

◇ Wave It High

I love to do large muscle movements with my students using ribbon wands. You can buy these commercially or make them by taping or gluing colorful ribbons to the end of a dowel or stick. As you wave them around in the air, they gently flow in the breeze. Another fun way to exercise these muscles is to give each student a plastic bag with hand-hole "handles"—the kind we get from the grocery store. Go outside, have each child grab both hand-holes in one hand, and run. They are trying to "catch the wind" and their plastic bag will billow and fly behind them. Once when we were doing this, there was a lull in the wind, and one child turned to me and said, "Well, Mrs. Rush, I think we got it all!" Have the children switch hands each time they make a run to catch the wind and hold the bag high for maximum muscle strengthening.

◇ Big Strokes for Big Folks

Ask the student to pretend that he or she is brushing a large set of teeth, like those of a dinosaur or giraffe. Using exaggerated movements, brush up and down and back and forth across the teeth, reaching high and bending low.

IDEAS FOR STUDENTS TO TRY:

Pretend to play tennis, using backhand and forehand swings, or pass a football.

Use a decorative wand to conduct music (see page 70).

Hold a piece of chalk in both hands and make circles on the blackboard; note which one is darker.

◇ Wash Day

Show your students how to pantomime the washing and scrubbing of clothes on a washboard, and hanging them out to dry. Do exaggerated twisting motions with your hands and arms as though you were wringing water out of a garment. Reach way down in the laundry basket to get the clothes and way up high to the clothesline to hang them, stretching from right to left and left to right.

◇ Rainbow Road

Mount a piece of 18" x 24" paper on an easel or blackboard. Draw a large, horizontal figure 8 on it. Have the child take a marker of every color and trace over the figure 8 with each one. This will create a "Rainbow Road." Then give the child a small Matchbox car to drive over the Rainbow Road. This is a great repetitive crossover activity.

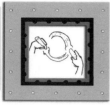

◇ Thumb Suckers

Keep an eye out for students who suck their thumb on one hand while working with the other. You will want to determine which hand is the more dominant and then work with the student to try to stop the thumb sucking. It is believed that continual thumb sucking can deform fingers, push the front teeth forward, and delay oral development.

IDEAS FOR STUDENTS TO TRY:

Mime the scrubbing or vacuuming of floors, or washing a large picture window.

"Play" the piano with both hands on a flat surface.

Pretend to drive a car with a gearshift, exaggerating the movements across the body when changing gears.

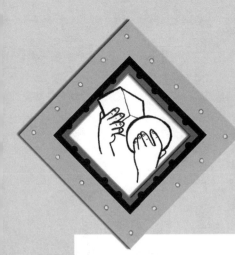

Tactile and Kinesthetic Learners

A lthough most teachers employ hands-on activities for some academic tasks, students who struggle may need even more instruction of this kind than we are providing— and on a regular basis. I try to work learning-by-doing into these students' daily routines and have found signing, story retellings, repetitive movements, and the other strategies included in this chapter to be particularly helpful.

◇ Sign Language

As you teach your students the alphabet, teach them the American Sign Language alphabet at the same time. It is perfect for tactile learners to see and feel each letter. A great visual resource for teaching this is *The Handmade Alphabet*, by Laura Rankin, published by Scholastic Inc. I bought two copies, pulled the pages apart, laminated them, and mounted the entire alphabet

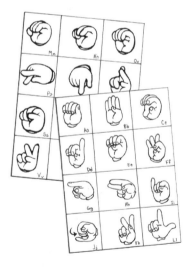

on my wall as an alphabet chart. The students love to stand next to it and form the signs for each letter. As I watch them I see them learning visually (by looking at the letter), auditorily (by saying the letter name and sound), and kinesthetically (by forming the hand sign).

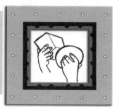

◇ Be the "B"

To get students interested in learning the alphabet make an alphabet book featuring each individual child. Use a digital camera to take a picture of the student (or of all the students in the class) creating the letters of the alphabet with his/her body. Children love to see themselves in action! (Check your school district's policy first, however, on parental permission to photograph students.)

◇ Falling into Place

Story sequencing is an important skill for fostering reading comprehension. Use a set of blocks (rectangular shape) to help tactile learners feel and see the  sequence of a story. After reading a book ask the students to draw pictures that show the events in the story, including the beginning, middle, and end. Mount these pictures (I tape them) onto blocks, with one picture per block. Stand up the blocks vertically and arrange them side by side, leaving about 3 inches between each one. As you retell the story according to the pictures, you can lay down each block as you get to that part. Then I have the students turn the blocks so

they look like dominoes lined up, and give a push to the first block, and the "story" falls into place before our eyes.

◇ Story Jar

To aid a child in retelling a story, I make a "story jar." I take a clean, clear plastic container, like a peanut butter jar, and fill it three-quarters full with sand. I then place small items inside that help to retell a familiar story. For example, for *The Three Little Pigs* I put in three little plastic pigs, a plastic wolf, and a few pieces of straw, twigs, and bits of red brick. The child rolls the jar and retells the story as the objects appear inside. He or she rolls the jar again until the next one shows, and so on. A variation is to affix a small magnetic strip to each piece and place them inside a coffee can. The student opens the can, takes out an item to use for the retelling, and then attaches it to the outside of the can by the magnetic strip.

IDEA TO TRY:

After your students have learned sign language, you can send silent signals to them—for example, to a student across the room during writing workshop who needs help spelling a word, or to a student whose behavior is disturbing others, etc.

◇ Silhouettes

Another way to help students with retelling a story is to have them draw one of the characters on a piece of oak tag (or you might want to draw the characters so they'll be more recognizable). Cut around the outline of the character and glue it onto a chopstick or long pencil. Turn on the overhead projector and use these cutouts to create silhouettes or shadow puppets to retell the story.

◇ Magnetic ABCs

Use a metal cookie sheet or baking pan and magnetic letters to teach alphabet recognition with kinesthetic learners. They can select letters, put them on the pan, and move them around to create words.

◇ Spell Check

I create a center for word recognition by using empty tin boxes from mints and magnetic letters. I cut a piece of paper the size of the front of the mint tin, write a word I want the student to learn on the paper, and attach it to the tin lid with book binding tape. Inside the tin I place the magnetic letters that spell the same word. The student looks at the word, opens the tin, and tries to arrange the letters to match. The student can recheck by looking at the cover.

◇ Say It with Feeling

Some students need to "feel" a word being sounded out along with hearing it. Use a Slinky toy for this. Hold the Slinky closed with both hands and say a word you want the student to learn. Then slowly stretch out the Slinky as you sound out the word. Repeat the procedure. Now pass the Slinky to your student, and let him/her go through the same motions while saying the word. Your students can do this exercise on their own repeatedly until they get the "feel" or sense of the word.

◇ Again and Again

Struggling learners benefit from seeing things over and over, but because they need tactile input as well, I use this method to reinforce letters, numbers, and words.

Write the letter "B" on the blackboard with a piece of chalk.

Ask the child to trace over the letter with the chalk while saying the letter "B."

Give the student a wet cotton ball to trace over the letter again, erasing it while repeating its name.

The image will remain briefly on the blackboard after it has been wiped away, so the student can then retrace the letter with the chalk and say the name again.

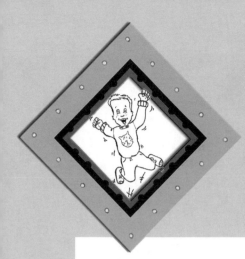

Hyperactivity

It amazes me how many students over the last 10 years have been diagnosed as having hyperactivity disorder. These children are in our classrooms yet we've been given very little information or instruction about how to help them maximize their learning as well as provide an appropriate outlet for their activity level. Be aware that later in life, they will be the adults whom everyone asks, "Where do you get all your energy?" or "How do you fit it all in?" Hyperactivity that is managed and understood can be a great asset.

◇ Up Against the Wall

If you have a student who climbs all over the others when sitting in a group or who acts up by touching or poking other children, have him or her sit next to a solid surface—like a wall or the side of a sturdy file cabinet or bookcase—so the shoulder, arm, and side of the body are in contact with that surface. This can help the child feel more secure and "grounded," and when he/she feels that way, you will notice that his/ her behavior improves.

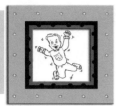

◇ A Special Place

Do you have a student who always pushes everyone else aside in order to be first in line? I have actually been knocked off balance by a child vying for the number one position. A good response to this kind of behavior is to designate a special place for that child in your class line. It doesn't necessarily have to be first, and the position can change daily or weekly. For example, I tell the student that he/she will be, say, fifth in line this week and then the next week I pick a new position. With this approach, the student is getting your attention and has a specific place to seek out, so the pushing should stop. This also provides an opportunity to teach ordinal numbers to the entire class!

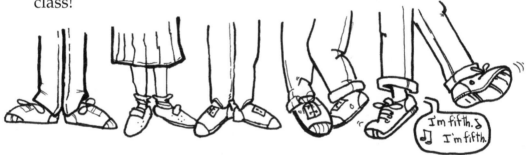

◇ Grounding

Some students have a neurological need to have weight on their bodies, which compresses joints and makes them feel grounded and more secure in their environment. You might try to provide this by simply resting your hand on the child's shoulder. This can provide comfort to a student who is feeling "out of control." Before touching any child, however, I recommend discussing this technique first with the parent. If a stu-

dent has a special education classification, an occupational therapist may suggest trying a "weighted vest." The student wears it for short periods of time during the day, and the amount of weight placed in the vest pockets is carefully calculated by the OT according to the student's weight. I also purchased a soft, plush play snake that is weighted and I allow any of the students to drape it around their neck  or shoulder area. It is reassuring and comforting to many of them.

◇ Draping

Some students need to have something draped over their heads (but with the face uncovered) in order to feel secure and "cocooned." I keep a flannel baby blanket (crib size is best) on hand and let the student wear it as a hooded cape. (Take it home and wash it after each use.) You can also accommodate this cocooning need  by allowing the student to wear his/her coat with the hood up, or even a removable coat hood. This will cut down on noise, too, which is an advantage for the child who is adversely affected by the volume of sound in the classroom.

◇ Fidgety vs. Stability

A student who continually falls off his/her chair can really disrupt the class, but a lot of fidgety students have a hard time sitting still. An occupational therapist can help you get a giant ball or a "T" seat for the student to sit on. This latter item, made of wood in a T-shape, requires the student to balance on it by sitting still. Of course the parent must be informed of this intervention in the student's Individual Education Plan. A nifty trick that has worked well for me with students who are not classified is to halfway inflate a child's swimming pool float or tube (the doughnut style). I place it in the child's chair and allow him/her to sit on top of it. This gets the wiggles out and keeps the child from "going overboard."

A similar trick is to have the student sit on a thick telephone book, which has been wrapped with duct tape so the covers and pages don't come apart. Surprisingly, the child doesn't fall off and it seems to define his/her space.

Ideas to Try:

Music can have a calming effect. Play soothing music in the background while students are working as a group, or allow a student to use a Walkman while working on an individual project.

Fluorescent lights can make a student agitated or hyper. Turn off a bank of overhead lights to see if that has a beneficial effect.

Note that odors and repetitive sounds can be disturbing and distracting to a hyperactive child. If the teacher next door is popping popcorn or someone is tapping a pencil on the table, these students may become irritated. Try to anticipate such possibilities and train yourself to notice even the smallest potential problem.

◇ Button Up

Some students have a hard time keeping their hands to themselves while sitting in a group. They are continually poking, touching, and bothering others. For these children I make a "button vest." I purchase an adult- or child-size vest from a thrift shop and sew a variety of buttons on the front, using embroidery or other thick thread. The fidgeting student can wear the vest and twist, twirl, and touch the buttons instead of the other students.

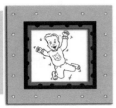

◇ Key Chain

Buy a key chain with a Koosh ball on the end of it and hang it on the belt loop of a fidgety child. Then the child can fiddle with the ball instead of bothering the students around him/her.

◇ In the Thick of Things

Sometimes I intentionally put the hyperactive student right in the middle of the action. If I am reading a big book, I let him or her hold one end of it and help me turn the pages. When we are doing a story retelling, I let him/her "be" the scenery. For example, the child can hold up his/her hands in the shape of a roofline to resemble a house for *The Three Little Pigs* or kneel down with hands on the floor to create a bridge for our puppets for the *Three Billy Goats Gruff*.

◇ Space-person

I enlist the help of a hyperactive student while I am putting my daily message, morning news, or group writing on the blackboard. He/she is my "space-person." Every time I finish writing a word, he/she can jump up and hold two fingers next to it so I can leave a two-finger space between that word and the next.

The student really has to concentrate on my writing demonstration to know when to come up. I allow all the students to take a turn with this, but it is the hyperactive child who needs the extra activity.

IDEAS TO TRY:

Make sure the hyperactive student has preferential seating near you.

Allow hyperactive students to be in motion while they are learning, and to have the option of working standing up, kneeling, or sitting.

Seat hyperactive students away from heavily trafficked areas.

◇ Rub Down

Many students need to learn a strategy that helps to calm themselves. A simple one is to have the student stroke the inside of his/her arm from the wrist to the elbow and back again, and then repeat the motion on the outside of the arm. You might also want to ask your occupational or physical therapist about "brushing," a technique they are trained to do with a soft, plastic brush, going up and down the arms and legs of a student. The parent must be informed of this first, of course, and agree to have it administered to his/her child by a trained professional. I have seen it work wonders on students!

◇ Rub It In

Another calming technique is to put a small drop of lotion in the palm of the student's hand and ask him/her to rub it on his/her hands and forearms while sitting on the carpet and listening to a story. I always check with the parent first to see if this will be okay, and I make sure the child doesn't have any allergies. I always use a hypoallergenic lotion that is suitable for baby skin.

IDEAS TO TRY:

Some students need to have something in their mouths or they will suck their thumb or shirt. Giving the child a clean toothbrush to chew on will satisfy "oral motor overflow desires," but never allow him/her to walk around with it in his or her mouth.

Having the student take deep breaths with the mouth slightly open will satisfy the need to have something touch the roof of the mouth and is a soothing relaxer for many.

Allow the hyperactive child plenty of space when he/she sits on the carpet or mat with other children.

◇ Standing Room Only

I designate a place in my classroom where students can stand and listen to a story or a lesson being taught. The rule is that they must pay attention, be quiet, and keep their hands to themselves. There are some hyperactive children who just cannot sit and learn—but standing works.

◇ Busy Body

Here is a silent solution to a foot-kicking problem. Take an exercise band (or a pair of old stockings) and wrap it around the front two legs of the student's chair. Make sure it is taut. The student then has two choices: keep his/her legs in front of the band and bounce the calves against it or place the legs in back of the band and bounce the shins against it. Either way he/she keeps legs and feet busy without kicking anyone.

◇ Kick-boxing

For students who cannot keep from kicking others under the table, I let them "practice" kick-boxing. I get a medium-size box, place it under the table, and have the student put his/her feet in it. That way the student kicks the box instead of someone else. To cut down on the noise, I line the inside with carpet remnants.

IDEAS TO TRY:

Check the hyperactive student's desk or table to make sure it is the right size or height for his/her body.

It is difficult for young students to sit on a hard chair for much more than 10 minutes at a time, and even harder for those who are hyperactive. So remember to get your students up from their seats about every 10 minutes to stretch and move around a bit.

Nonverbal/Shyness

$\mathbf{I}$t is difficult for a teacher to assess a student who is nonverbal or very shy. If the child won't speak, how can you find out what he/she knows? You have to assume that the student understands some of the information being taught, but without some kind of feedback, doing an assessment can be a real challenge. This chapter focuses on ways to gain these students' trust, encourage communication, and inspire participation in the classroom.

◇ Preview

If you have learned from a parent or by prescreening that a very shy or nonverbal student is going to be in your class, invite that child to visit your classroom before the school year begins. To ensure that he/she really feels comfortable, the student should visit three separate times: one month, one week, and one day before school starts. I always

show the student the dress I will wear the first day and this also seems to reduce the child's anxiety level.

◇ Breeze Through

The day before school begins I invite all students to come and "breeze through" the classroom, and I designate a half-hour time period for this. I also ask that the parent(s) and student come into the school by the entrance he/she will use the following day, walk down the hallway, and enter the classroom, taking a quick look around. I meet and greet them, wearing the same dress that I'll have on the next day, the first day of school. Then they walk back up the hall and out the door for home. I remember a time when a student said the following day, "I know you—I saw you yesterday!"

◇ Ask Me About It

I use this strategy to encourage talking at home and at school. On half a sheet of paper, I write a few words pertaining to a specific topic or something that happened in school that day. I send it home with the student and include a request that the parent do the same on the other half of the paper—write a word or two about something that happened at home. I don't write a narrative and don't want the parent to either. Instead, I want the student to verbalize the details about the words we wrote down. When the student brings the paper home, the

parent will talk to the child about his/her day and the related topic. When I get the paper back, I will be able to initiate a discussion with the student based on what the parent wrote. I have learned many wonderful things about students with this approach. It is a springboard for discussion as well as a good way to prompt a student who doesn't know what to write about at journal writing time.

◇ Puppet Pals

Some shy students have a hard time looking me—or anyone else—in the eye, so I use puppets to talk to them and I ask the students to respond to the puppet. The puppet is funny, reassuring, and compassionate, which helps the student feel more relaxed. I take a cloth puppet and put my picture on it. I move the puppet away from my face and converse with the student while using the puppet. As often as possible, I move the puppet back toward my face so the student can see my facial expressions but doesn't have to look me directly in the eye. My goal with this technique is to have the puppet right next to my face and then eventually remove the puppet altogether and have the child talk directly to me face-to-face.

IDEA TO TRY:

Be aware that some students dislike being touched; even a tap on the shoulder can be disturbing. Keep this in mind when seating these students with their classmates.

 ## Do-Re-Mi

Do lots of singing! Music and singing are contagious and fully engage the brain. Most students love to sing and feel a sense of freedom while doing so. Sometimes I have a student who is too shy to sing so I hand him/her a "conductor's wand" (a chopstick that I dipped the top third in glue and then sprinkled with glitter to make it look magical). Before long he/she is joining in on the singing too!

◇ Look Me Right in the Sticker

For a child who is very shy and has a hard time meeting your eyes, try putting a sticker on your face. You can put it on your chin, cheek, nose, or forehead. Ask the child to look at the sticker while he/she talks to you. That way he/she can see your facial expressions. This may be the first step in getting the child to lift up his/
her head and "read" your face and facial expressions. Looking at a person when he/she talks to you is an important life skill.

◇ Courage

Give the shy student a "courage" ball. I use a colored puffball that is small enough to slip into the child's hand and be concealed there. I tell the child that this ball will help him/her face new things that will be happening that day.

◇ Rainy Days

Be aware that when air pressure is low, students may need some private quiet time. Turn off a bank of lights in the classroom, turn on some soothing music, and have the students sit quietly for a few minutes.

IDEA TO TRY:

Provide a fan to keep air circulating in the classroom, but make sure to keep it and its electrical cord out of reach of the students.

◇ Silent Response Signals

If you have students who like to raise their hands so they can be like the rest of the children, but they don't really want to be called on to answer your question, you can show them some "silent response signals." For example, thumbs up can mean "yes" and thumbs down can mean "no," or arms crossed, "agree" and uncrossed, "disagree." For those who need extra processing time, I tell them that if they raise their hand and leave it open and extended, I won't call on them until they give me the signal that they are ready by closing their hand into a fist. That way they are signaling to me that they "have the answer right here in my hand (and my head)."

IDEAS TO TRY:

Students can absorb more if they are sitting comfortably, so have cushions or mats for the floor, or a carpeted area in your classroom.

Allow a child plenty of space when he/she sits on the carpet or mat with other children.

 ## Freedom with Information

I encourage students to use any resource that will help them find an answer to their question. If this means looking at another student's paper for direction, then I openly encourage it. I don't want to have students perfect the art of cheating by giving a sly sideways glance and hide the fact that they need help. I invite them to walk around the room and look at other students' work or find resources (like the number line or word wall) for help with whatever they are stuck on. If I have an assessment that requires a student to work completely independently, I always make sure it is understood that this time the stu-  dent is on his/her own. I let students know that they should try their very best and that all their efforts are great.

◇ "Be" the Scenery

For someone extremely shy, I will let the child "be" the scenery in a play or a story retelling. That way the child is involved in the action without having to speak. For example, the student could hold hands with another student and "be" the bridge for *The Three Billy Goats Gruff.* My goal is to help the child become involved and enjoy the experience so much that the next time he/she will want to say a line or participate more in the play or retelling.

◇ Echo Answers

Sometimes, when I ask a question and get an answer from one student, I give all the others in class a chance to echo or call out the same thing. This way the correct answer or information gets repeated over and over again. There is no risk involved and a shy child can chime in without fear of being singled out. For example, I might ask, "Who can spell the word 'this'?" After a student spells it correctly, I will ask if anyone else can spell it and I keep calling on anyone

who wants to spell it. Often, by the time 10 or so students have responded, the shy child feels comfortable enough to speak up too.

◇ Looking Ahead

It is helpful for a child to know what is coming up in the next grade. Make a list of what will happen the following school year and include fun things the child can look forward to. If you want to get fancy, you could ask a parent, aide, or paraprofessional to make a videotape—for example, "A Day in the Life of a First Grader." I always ask a former student (who is now a first  grader) to come to my kindergarten room near the end of each school year to tell about the great things that happen in first grade. You can do something similar for parents too. Ask an "alumni" parent to meet with parents of the upcoming class to answer questions and talk about the next grade level. (Carefully choose the parent who will be the best representative for your programs at school.)

◇ Fair Warning

I forewarn children who are shy and afraid of sudden changes when we will be switching activities. I might say, "In five minutes we will____" or "We are just about ready to____" or "Now we are going to ____." This gives the child the security of knowing what comes next.

> In five minutes we will be going to the library.

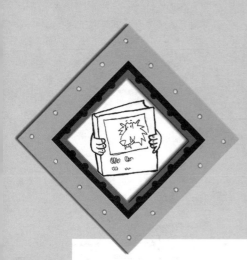

Book-handling Skills

Many struggling learners enter school with little or no experience with books. This means that you will need to get books into their hands right from the start. But sharing your much-loved books with inexperienced students can spell disaster. I have had children virtually destroy books by biting, chewing, and tearing the pages. This was not done out of malicious intent but because they had never had the opportunity to hold, handle, and interact with books. Because of this lack of exposure, they often need direct instruction regarding book-handling skills.

◇ Board Books

Children's book publishers are offering more and more "board books," (those with hard cardboard pages). Traditionally made as "baby books," they now include "big kid" titles too. These board books facilitate easier page turning practice and stand up well to the rough handling of young readers.

◇ Ziploc Books

Write each letter of the alphabet on a 5"x 5" piece of oak tag. Give one to each student and ask him/her to draw on the back side a picture of something that begins with the letter they have. (You may need to help give ideas for some of the letters like q, x, y, z.) When they finish, slip each piece into a separate quart-size Ziploc bag, arrange them in alphabetical order, and staple all the bags together to form a book. (I put tape over the staples so no one snags a finger on the sharp metal ends.) The book is sturdy, stands up to rough handling, and stays clean because the pages can be wiped off.

◇ Cereal Box Books

These books will make your students feel right at home. I cut off the front cardboard panel of popular children's cereal boxes and bind them together in book form. This creates a very durable book that is popular with all the students because it is bright and colorful, and they are already familiar with the logos and print. The student learns how to properly hold a book because he or she can easily tell if it is upside down, and no print or picture will show if it is turned backwards. I use this as a teaching tool

for alphabet recognition too. Most cereal labels are printed in uppercase block letters which can be used to help students pick out the letters in their names and to learn new letters, too.

◇ Favorites

Always buy two copies of your most loved books—especially if they are paperbacks. Keep one copy in your teacher collection so it does not get "over loved" by the students and will stay nice for many years. I actually buy three or four copies of my class favorites because these books go through so many little hands. I use one copy to tear apart the pages, laminate, and put in a large Ziploc bag so the students can use it to retell a story. They remove the pages from the bag, lay them out, and retell the story in their own words. You can do this as an independent activity or as a class project. For the latter, I put the pages of the book out of order on the ledge of the blackboard. After reading the book many times we decide which picture goes first, which comes next, and so on.

IDEAS TO TRY:

Show the student how to hold a book so it is right side up with the cover facing him/her.

Demonstrate how to respect a book by handling it with care and not bending the pages. Show the student how to turn the pages one at a time.

◇ All About Me

One of the best techniques for practicing book-handling skills is to write a book *about* the student. I generate a story on the computer, with the help of the child, and print it out. The student then illustrates each page. I laminate the pages and bind them into a book. I have found that the student respects his/her book, and book-handling problems all but disappear because the child has full ownership of the precious book.

IDEAS TO TRY:

Point out what is on the title page, dedication page, and copyright page and explain that this text is not directly involved with the story.

Point out where the print is located on each page and where to begin reading. Explain how the pictures help the reader understand what the words on the page say.

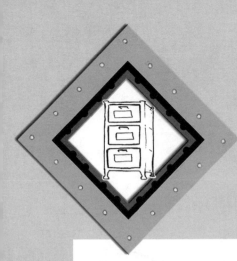

Organizational Issues

Students in the early grades often need help with getting organized. Generally, these are the children who have their belongings strewn all over the classroom or work space by the end of the school day. We need to help them learn strategies to organize their personal space and navigate through their day without falling apart. This will be a daily challenge that must be addressed before learning can take place.

◇ Where Am I?

Students who have a hard time getting organized can never seem to find the workbook page that they are supposed to be on. Often it takes them so long that the rest of the class will have finished the assignment

before they've even begun! Here's a quick fix: Have them cut off the corner of the page that was just completed. That way the student simply locates the next page that has not been cut. If he or she is not yet able to use scissors correctly, cut it off yourself or have the student fold down the corner.

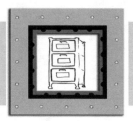

◇ Count by Tens

Put a colored tab on every tenth page of the student's workbook. That way the child can tell at a glance where, say, page 50 is and then use that marker to find page 52. This works well for children who recognize numbers, but for those who don't, just color code your tabs so you know what pages they represent. Then you can say, "Turn to the pages marked by the red tab."

◇ Bookmark

Use a sticky note to mark the next workbook page to be used. Each time a student finishes one page, he/she removes the note and sticks it on the next page. Remind the child to place the note upside down so the tacky part sticks to the page and the opposite end protrudes above the page to serve as a bookmark.

◇ Picture This

Take pictures of any routine that you want the student to accomplish on a daily basis. For example, at the very beginning of the year, I photograph the students completing all the daily tasks, like unpacking their backpacks, putting papers in the basket, getting a new reading book, hanging up their coats, etc. I then put the pictures in sequential order and hang them prominently so all can see the daily routine. If a student is having a hard time with a routine, we take a "picture walk" as we talk through the right steps. My aide developed one for showing students the correct procedure for washing and drying their hands before leaving the bathroom. Those photos are right next to the sink. (Remember to check first on your school district's policy regarding photographing students.)

◇ Spic-and-Span

I also take pictures of every area of my classroom the day before school starts. This is after I have spent a great amount of time cleaning and organizing the entire space. I mount each picture by the matching area with a sign that reads "THIS IS A CLEAN HOUSE CENTER" or "THIS IS A CLEAN BLOCKS CENTER" or "THIS IS A CLEAN READING CENTER." Later, when I ask the students to "clean up," they know how the center is supposed to look. (Not that it ever really looks like that again, but one can always hope!)

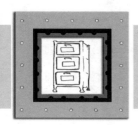

◇ Personal Trashcans

I have many students who can pick up their scraps when they have finished an art project but they have lots of trouble getting them all to the trashcan. So, for messy projects I put "personal" trashcans on each table or cluster of desks. These are made from large-size (2 lb.) coffee cans covered with brightly colored Con-Tact paper. The students put all their trash in these table-top containers when they are through with the work and an assigned student gathers them up and empties each one into the classroom trashcan. Another way to keep things neat is to have a student circulate around the classroom two or three times a day with one of these personal trashcans to collect scraps that students have found near their desks.

◇ Stick It to It

Velcro comes in handy when teaching a child with organizational difficulties. Put a strip of it near your meeting or circle-time area (on the chalk ledge of the blackboard, for example) so that as you discuss your schedule for the upcoming day, you can attach pictures to the strip to show what will be happening in the order of its occurrence. I like to take pictures of the students involved in each activity of the day so they can see themselves doing our daily work. (Always check first to see what your school district's policy is on photographing students.) You can also attach a few pieces of Velcro to the child's desk and use them to place pictures of the order of work to be done, like "color, cut, paste." Or take pictures from the class schedule and

place them on the child's personal schedule to show what is coming next. This has the additional benefit of giving the child advance notice of an upcoming transition.

◇ Shadow

There is nothing better for organizational issues than to have a child shadow a peer. Being able to "see" things in action helps the student learn how to complete tasks by him/herself. *You* can show the student too, of course, but it is even better (and more fun) for the child to learn from a peer.

◇ Flip It Up

Some students need a resource or reminder right at their fingertips so I make a mini pop-up card for them. Take an index card, fold it in half crosswise, and cut two parallel lines, centered, across the folded edge. The cuts are about ½ inch apart and about 1 inch long. Open the card and pull out the cut section so it forms a 90° angle. From another index card, cut out a small square or rectangle shape, and write on it the letter or word a student is struggling with. Glue this to the front face of the 90° angle, close the card, folding down the top half, and secure the bottom of the card to the child's desk. Then, the child simply flips up the card whenever he/she needs to take a peek at the letter or word written there.

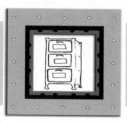

IDEAS TO TRY:

Limit the number of personal belongings that can be brought to school.

Designate a place where the student can put his/her belongings, like a personal cubby, an individual coat hook, or a bag hooked onto his/her chair.

Schedule short "reorganization" times during the day for the student to take a moment to gather his/her stuff and put it in its proper place.

 ## A Place to Call Their Own

Give students a special place where they can lay out things. This could be a small section of a bookshelf or an additional cubby space. If pencils, scissors, glue, and other "tools" for the day are spread out in clear view, your students will have an easier time finding things. That way, when you are ready for the class to start a writing lesson, art project,

or some other activity, these students also will be ready.

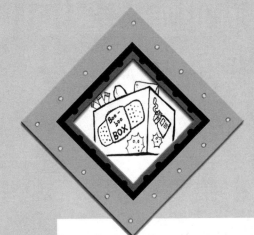

Other Issues

Over the years I have noticed that some students who struggle occasionally stretch the truth or become what I call "Frequent Flyers" to the nurse's office. If they are making something up (like pretending to be sick), they are not only taking time away from academic tasks but may also be trying to run away from a problem or a lesson that is difficult for them. I want them to know that they can always come to me for help. Here are some strategies I use for getting to the heart of the matter.

 ## Tough Times

Sometimes a student will say something that isn't true because life is tough for him/her. I ignore what has been said and ask the child, "What is the hardest thing about being you?" I have found that this shows that I know the child is stretching the truth but I also know that he/she is a worthwhile person and I am willing to listen to anything he/she has to say. This one question can open up a floodgate of emotions that can explain a lot about why the child may be untruthful at times.

Offer an Out

If a student persists in stretching the truth, I give him/her a chance to start all over. I say that I am going to walk a few steps away and empty out my ears. Then when I come back with "fresh ears," the student can start again and tell the truth. My "new ears" will never remember what was said earlier.

To Tell the Truth

Because of their home life, some students may have gotten into a pattern of stretching the truth as a survival skill to avoid punishment. You want your students to feel safe in your classroom and retain their dignity and credibility. So, when a student denies doing something that you know he or she did do, ask him or her, "Did you do it *just a little bit*?" This allows the student to tell the truth without having to give in completely until he/she knows that you are a safe haven for truthfulness.

Three Bears

When I know that a student has not been truthful, I don't even bother asking if he/she is telling the truth because that provides another opportunity for not being truthful. Instead, I simply ask if it is a "big truth-stretching," a "medium truth-stretching," or a "baby/little truth-stretching." That way I offer an opportunity for the child to begin telling the truth.

◇ Me Too

When I listen to a student who is not telling the truth, I will tell him or her about a situation from my own childhood that may be somewhat similar to what is going on now. I say that I could have lied about it but decided to tell the truth. I let the child know that he/she can tell me anything and that I was little once, too!

IDEAS TO TRY:

When asking a child "Why did you do [or say] that?" really listen for what is NOT being said and watch the child's nonverbal cues to see what can be read from his/her body language. The child may be trying to communicate that "nobody likes me" or "a bully is picking on me and I'm afraid," etc.

Sometimes a child feels that he/she must say something spectacular rather than slight or trivial. I let these things pass because it is part of the age/stage of young children.

◇ Frequent Flyers

Sometimes a struggling learner will pretend to feel bad so he or she can "escape" to the nurse's office. Generally, you will be able to determine if the student is truly sick or just needs to be noticed and provided some TLC. In order to cut down on the number of "Frequent-Flyer" trips to the nurse, you might suggest first that the child use the bathroom, lie down for a while, or take a drink of water. I also keep the following on hand: Band-Aids—the brighter and more pictures, the better; a cold compress; and an ice pack.

IDEAS TO TRY:

Let the child rub some glitter lotion (lotion with some sparkles in it) where he/she hurts, as long as it is not on the face, because it could get in the eyes.

Apply a little dab of "boo-boo paste" (Vaseline) to the area that aches or feels painful.

AFTERWORD

Change is hard. It doesn't make a difference whether you're five or fifty, change is hard. We, as teachers, are by our very nature "change agents." We spend our entire career teaching students to be better, brighter, and the best they can be. I know that I always want to make a change for the better when I find a student struggling. But I always remind myself that change is hard.

To keep me mindful of this, I do a simple exercise: I clasp my hands together with fingers interlocked and my thumbs crossed at the top. Then I redo the grasp by repositioning the fingers so that the other thumb is on top. Try it! Doesn't it feel completely uncomfortable and foreign to you? Now imagine that each school day a teacher is going to ask you to clasp your hands together, expecting you to do it the second way, not the first. You would be confused and 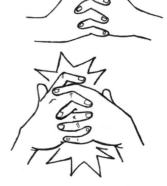 frustrated most of the time. So whenever I want to try to change a student's current way of doing things, I clasp my hands together, the awkward way, and this keeps me mindful and more patient.

Now imagine that I ask you day after day to make another change. How long do you think it would take to start feeling comfortable with the change? I don't know about you, but I want a change to work immediately! Unfortunately, that's not how it is. You need to keep up a behavior for 6 to 12 weeks before you start to see a change occurring. This goes for children as well as adults. If I want to lose weight, it will require 6 to 12 weeks of dieting before I see a significant difference; if I want to be in better physical condition, it will take 6 to 12 weeks before I notice the benefits of exercising. If I want a student to change his/her pencil grip, I need to work with that student for 6 to 12 weeks. This 6- to 12-week period will make change part of regular behavior.

It is also important that you work on only one change at a time and record the outcome of the change. If you try to make several changes at once, you will not know which one worked and which one did not at the end of the 6- to 12-week period. Choose the one behavior/habit that you think will most benefit the student and work on that one only.

Change can be fun, though, and you can make it that way by presenting it as such. I know a kindergarten teacher who teaches tying shoes and then celebrates the ability to do so by giving the student a pair of rainbow-colored shoelaces. Think outside the box for ways to make change fun. Take a picture of the child (checking first, of course, on the school district's policy regarding photographing students) and write a caption on the photograph, which might read, "Caught you making a change for the better!" Keep a flashlight handy and shine it on a child who is really trying hard to learn a new task to "spotlight" this positive change.

It is imperative that you remain objective as you approach the challenge of teaching struggling learners. You need to remember that some of these students are very literal in their thinking. They may have trouble with the hypothetical; change and new experiences may cause great anxiety. Often these students are stuck in one world or one way of thinking. We can help them by habituating their changes and allowing them to do something over and over again before we ask them to perform the task well. They may lack flexibility, so we need to be even more flexible to accommodate the differences. Give the students many chances to show off the talents they do have.

Be tender with parents of a student who struggles. It can take years for parents to finally come to grips with the fact that their child struggles in school. It is very akin to the grief process. Many parents will need as much support as their child does. Give it to them and give it with love. You may not get far in one year but you will have planted a seed for acceptance and celebration of the child and his/her uniqueness. Every child can learn and grow.

And last of all, be easy on yourself. At the end of a day of trying your hardest and doing your very best, go out to dinner, go for a jog, or take a long hot bath. Make sure you treat yourself well and you will have the energy to do it all again tomorrow. Celebrate the unique gifts that you provide to all students but especially to those who struggle each and every day.

INDEX